DATE DUE			

Action Sports Library

Skateboarding

Bob Italia

Published by Abdo & Daughters, 6535 Cecilia Circle, Edina, Minnesota 55439.

Library bound edition distributed by Rockbottom Books, Pentagon Tower, P.O. Box 36036, Minneapolis, Minnesota 55435.

Printed in the United States.

ISBN: 1-56239-077-5

Library of Congress Card Catalog Number: 91-073020

Cover Photos: ©ALLSPORT USA/PHOTOGRAPHER, 1991.
Inside Photos: ©ALLSPORT USA/PHOTOGRAPHER, 1991.

Warning: The series *Action Sports Library* is intended as entertainment for children. These sporting activities should never be attempted without the proper conditioning, training, instruction, supervision, and equipment.

Edited by Rosemary Wallner

CONTENTS

Skateboarding—it's not what it used to be!

SKATEBOARDING

The Story of the Board

Skateboarding became popular in southern California in the early 1960s. Surfers saw that they could practice their surfing techniques on skateboards when surfing conditions were not good.

By 1965, skateboarding fever had spread across the country. Nearly 50 million skateboards were sold. But by the end of that year, skateboarding was already on the decline. Many people did not like the quality of the skateboards being made. The wheels, usually made of steel, did not grip street surfaces well and would lock when they struck a stone or pebble. The boards were thick and stiff and would not absorb shock from bumps.

It took almost 10 years before a new kind of skateboard appeared on the market. The steel wheels were replaced with urethane plastic wheels. These wheels had outstanding gripping power. They could absorb shock better and roll over stones and pebbles. And the plastic wheels allowed smooth, sharp turns.

Improvements on the board were made, too. The boards were longer, wider, and thinner, which allowed for more cushion and maneuverability. They had a roughened deck for surefooting. And with the addition of the railbars and curved kick tail, tricks could be performed.

All these improvements added up to a renewed interest in skateboarding. By 1975, skateboarding fever once again swept the country. Magazines such as *Skateboarder* and *Skateboard* hit the market. And skateboard ramps began appearing everywhere. Today, skateboarding is more popular than ever.

The Modern Skateboard

It's important to know the components of a skateboard so proper maintenance can be performed. The modern skateboard is made up of:

- The deck (where you stand).
- The kick tail (the curved end used for quick turns and tricks).
- Railbars (located beneath the board and used for tricks on the lip of the ramps).
- The trucks (the steel mechanisms that fasten the wheels to the board and allow them to turn).
- The ball bearings (which allow the wheels to spin smoothly).
- The wheels.

Get in the habit of checking your skateboard before you use it. Make sure the railbars are fastened tightly to the bottom of the board. Tighten the screws that fasten the trucks to the board.

The most important part of skateboard maintenance is wheel inspection. Make sure there are no flat spots on the wheels. Now spin the wheels. If the wheels come to an abrupt stop, the bearings may be dirty. Use a bearing spray to remove the dirt. You can buy bearing spray at most sporting goods stores. The wheels may also be too tight. Try loosening the bearing nut in the center of the wheel. If the wheels wobble, use your skate key to tighten the truck bolt.

Now give your skateboard a slight push. If the board doesn't roll in a straight line, the truck bolt may be bent. Rather than risk injury, take the board into a shop where it can be repaired by a professional.

To get the most out of your wheels, make sure you rotate them every four weeks. Follow this rotating pattern:

• front left to right rear;
• front right to left rear;

•left rear to front right;
•right rear to front left.

You will also want to check your board. Although they are very durable, extended use can cause cracks. Slight cracks can be repaired by a professional. Deep or wide cracks are cause for concern, and the board should be replaced.

A little preventive maintenance will keep you safe, preserve your board, and help you enjoy the sport.

Skateboarding Styles

Before choosing a skateboard, it's important to determine what kind of skateboarding you'll be doing.

There are three types of skateboarding styles:

- Freestyle—The skateboarder skates across a smooth, flat surface and performs tricks.

- Streetstyle—The skateboarder skates over ramps and performs tricks.

- Racing Style—The skateboarder races downhill or through a slalom course of plastic cones.

Once you've chosen the kind of skateboarding you're interested in, select the proper type of skateboard wheel. There are two kinds:

- The Standard Wheel—These wheels are 1.125 inches thick and 1.5 inches in diameter. They are best suited for beginners and freestyle skateboarding. They do not grip the surface well at high speeds.

- Extra-Large Wheels—These wheels are 2.25 inches thick and 2.625 inches in diameter.

They are best suited for downhill speed racing. Since the board rides high with these wheels, it makes freestyle skating more difficult.

You may also want to make sure that the bearings are *double-sealed* precision ball bearings. They are more expensive than the *single-sealed* and *open* ball bearings, but they have their advantages. Double-sealed ball bearings give a smoother, quieter, and more stable ride. They won't wobble at high speeds, they last longer, and they require no maintenance.

In the 1970s and early 1980s, the flexboard was the most popular deck design. Flexboards were made of fiberglass, plastic, or aluminum. But now, a new type of wooden board has become more popular. It is made of several layers of wood (usually oak, maple, or beech). It is just as flexible as a flexboard, but is more sturdy and lightweight, and can absorb shocks very well.

Take a look at the trucks as well. If they are mounted close to the tips of the board, this will give you a long wheelbase. A long wheelbase is best suited for downhill skateboarding. If the trucks are mounted closer towards the center, this is called a short wheelbase. A short wheelbase is best suited for freestyle skateboarding. Choose the board that is best for your type of skateboarding.

Accessories

You may want to buy some skateboard accessories to add to the life of your skateboard:

- Tailplate—This metal plate is placed across the bottom of the kicktail and protects the back of the board from being worn and damaged.

- Nose guard—This is made of urethane or rubber and is placed across the nose (front tip) of the board, protecting it from damage.

- Curb hopper—This is attached to the front or rear truck and helps the skateboarder over curbs and other obstacles.

- Coper—This plastic device fits on the truck axles, protecting them from wear.

- Railbars—These plastic strips are placed lengthwise along the bottom edges of the board. They are used for stunts and make the board stronger and more durable.

Wearing the proper clothes and safety equipment will cut down on injuries. Long pants are recommended—jeans offer the best protection against knee scrapes. Long sleeve shirts or sweatshirts will protect your elbows and forearms.

When skateboarding, always wear rubber-soled shoes that don't have heels. They won't jab you when you fall, and they offer the best gripping power. Make sure your laces are tied tightly and aren't dangling over the sides of the board.

Padded gloves, helmets, and knee and elbow pads are also recommended. They can be bought at most sporting goods stores. The best kind of helmet is a bicycle helmet. They should be worn especially if you are a downhill racer. It only takes one tumble to appreciate the protective qualities of this equipment.

Where to Go

There are many places you can go to safely enjoy skateboarding. A popular place is the private driveway. A dead-end street is also a good place to skateboard. If you live near a school, try the playground. Any of these places are good as long as they have smooth surfaces and are free of traffic.

Skateboard parks are the ultimate choice for skateboarders. Unfortunately, there are not many in existence. A skateboard park has a variety of ramps, slopes, flat surfaces, and race courses for skateboarders to practice and learn skateboarding techniques. Park supervisors and instructors can teach you to become a better skateboarder.

You may also want to consider a summer skateboard camp. They also offer professional instruction and a variety of safe skateboarding courses. Most skateboarding camps last between three and six weeks. Find out all you can about the camps from other skateboarders who have attended them, or from skateboarding clubs, organizations, or associations.

Some Basic Safety Rules

To get the most enjoyment out of skateboarding, follow these basic safety rules:

• Never cross an intersection on your skateboard.

- Don't show off.

- Never skateboard into the street from behind a parked car.

- Never ride through puddles or on wet or sandy pavement. The plastic wheels won't grip when they're wet, and sand can damage the bearings.

- Never do stunts or ride down hills or around obstacles unless you have practiced and feel comfortable.

- Learn how to fall.

The most important safety rule is learn how to fall. Even professionals know how to take a tumble. Falling is part of skateboarding. Learning how to fall can mean the difference between embarrassment and injury.

The closer you are to the ground, the less chance you will be injured. When you feel yourself losing control, try to lower your body and roll off the board. Cover your eyes with one arm and tumble—preferably into a grassy area.

Scrapes and bruises are the most common injuries. Scrapes should be cleaned and patched up to prevent infection. If a fracture occurs, try not to move and call for help. Moving a person who is seriously injured can make the injury even worse.

Learning How to Skateboard

Lessons are available and recommended, but not necessary. You can learn the basics of skateboarding by observing skateboarding friends.

Place one foot on the board and slowly push with the other. Practice this for a while until you get a good feel for the board. Then try placing the other foot on the board. Don't place your feet too closely to, or far apart from, each other. You won't feel comfortable, and it will affect your balance.

A proper stance involves comfort and balance. Try different stances. Keep your front foot pointed slightly forward. Hold your arms out in front of you and bend your knees slightly. Most importantly, look straight ahead, not down.

When you feel comfortable gliding on your skateboard, you're ready to try some turns. Lower your body closer to the ground. Twist your shoulders and hips in the direction you want to go. The more you lean in the direction of the turn, the sharper the turn will be. Try not to turn too suddenly. This may cause you to lose you balance. When you've completed your turn, return your body to the gliding position with knees slightly bent and weight evenly distributed in the center of the board.

To stop the board, first slow down. Then remove the back foot and then the front foot.

Freestyle Skateboarding

Once you've mastered the basic skateboarding techniques, you may want to try freestyle skateboarding. There are many types of freestyle stunts. Many can be mastered with just a little practice (bring a friend along in case of an injury). These are the most popular stunts:

- One-foot nose wheelie—Place your front foot on the front end of the board and allow the back wheels to rise.

- One-foot tail wheelie—Place your back foot on the tail of the board and allow the front wheels to rise.

- Handstand wheelie—Do a handstand on the board and allow the front or back wheels to rise.

When doing wheelies, keep your balance over the wheels that remain on the pavement. Tail wheelies are easier than nose wheelies, so you may want to try them first. Remember, if you don't feel comfortable doing any of these stunts, stop and get off the board. It's not worth risking an injury.

Another basic and popular stunt is the *kickturn*. Put one foot on the rear of the board and the other towards the front. Then push down on the tail. When the nose lifts, direct it with your front foot. When you complete your turn, allow the front wheels to return to the pavement.

When you feel comfortable with the kickturn, try a *360-turn*— turning in a complete circle with the front or rear wheels in the air. A 360-turn requires excellent balance. The more you practice, the better you will become.

The *Ollie* is an advanced freestyle stunt. It allows the board to rise completely off the ground—as if it were flying!

Performing the *Ollie* over a canyon.

Press your rear foot on the tail. When the front of the board rises, slide your front foot from the middle to the tip of the board. The board will then leap off the ground. Keep your knees bent and your arms extended. This will help you keep your balance and absorb the shock of landing.

The *fingerflip* is performed by crouching and placing both feet on the tail of the board. When the front wheels rise, grab the tip of the board and jump into the air. Then land on the board with both feet.

Jumping

Skateboard jumping is the most exciting and spectacular of the skateboard stunts. It requires the most practice, timing, and proper balance. Never attempt skateboard jumps unless you feel comfortable with the stunts. Here are the most popular jumping tricks:

- Board-to-board jumping—Most experts recommend that the board-to-board jump be the first jump stunt you attempt. To perform the stunt, you'll need two skateboards. Crouching, ride one board towards the other that has been placed ahead of you. When you've just about reached the other board, jump from your board and try to land in the middle of the other board. Make sure you bend your knees when you land to absorb the shock. Then move your feet to a proper gliding stance.

- Barrel jumping—This is an advanced version of the board-to-board jump. To set it up, find some barrels or garbage cans, lay them on their sides, and line them up in a row. Use as many barrels as you feel comfortable with. Place the second skateboard on the opposite end of the barrels, then make your run. When you reach the barrels, crouch and spring from the board. Keep your knees bent as you soar over the barrels, then land in the middle of the second board.

Skateboard Ramps

There are many types of ramps used in streetstyle skating. Three of the most popular ramps are the quarterpipe, the halfpipe, and the jump. These ramps are usually made out of wood. The jump ramp has the simplest design. The quarterpipe and halfpipe ramps are much larger and require the bending of plywood to obtain their curved surfaces.

Performing a stunt on a halfpipe.

The skateboarder skates forwards and backwards on a quarterpipe or halfpipe ramp and performs stunts on the lip of the ramps. These stunts are called *lip tricks*. The jump ramp is used for jump stunts.

The *handplant* is a favorite stunt performed on a ramp. When skateboarders reach the lip of the ramp, they grip the lip of the ramp with one hand and the board with the other. The skateboarders then do a hand stand on the lip while holding their skateboards to their feet. Then the skateboarders return the board to the ramp with both feet on their boards.

Slalom Racing

If you're not interested in stunts, you may want to try slalom racing. All you need is a hill or ramp and some objects to skate around. When starting out, don't be concerned about speed. Work on your turning ability and see if you can steer around all the slalom course obstacles. Once you've mastered the course, try to see how fast you can complete the run.

Slalom racing tests your ability to turn quickly.

Downhill Racing

Downhill racing presents the greatest challenge to skateboarders—not because of the difficulty, but because of the dangerous speeds attained. Some expert downhill skateboarders have reached speeds of 60 miles an hour and faster. Falling during one of these runs can cause serious injury—even death.

When attempting a downhill run, assume a crouching position and keep your arms extended. Keep both feet towards the middle of the board and pointing forward. And *always* wear protective clothing and equipment—especially a helmet. *Never* attempt a downhill run unless you have outstanding skateboarding skills and excellent board control.

Skateboard Associations

Once you've mastered the skateboard and its many forms and stunts, you may want to try organized competitions. To do this, check the telephone book for the nearest skateboard association. You can also write to the following addresses for more information:

- National Skateboard Association
  P.O. Box 3645
  San Bernardino, CA 92413

- Eastern Skateboarding Association
  101 Warren Avenue
  Seekonk, MA 02771

- Canadian Amateur Skateboard Association
  15791 Columbia Avenue
  White Rock, British Columbia, Canada
  VHB 1L6

These associations will keep you informed of all the skateboarding events in your area.

Skateboard competitions are held
all over the world.

Some also have memberships that offer T-shirts, newsletters, and decals.

A Final Word

Skateboarding is one of the most exciting and rewarding sports for today's young people. Remember, always be careful when you're out and about on your skateboard. Wear the proper clothing and equipment, and never attempt a run or a stunt if you don't feel comfortable. Follow these simple safety rules, and you'll get the most enjoyment out of skateboarding.

GLOSSARY

- Ball bearings—steel balls in the skate board wheels that allow them to turn smoothly.

- Deck—the flat surface of the skateboard.

- Flexboard—a type of skateboard made of fiberglass or plastic that bends to absorb shock.

- Freestyle—a skateboarding style that uses stunts.

- Kicktail—the curved back end of the skateboard.

- Racing style—a skateboarding style used on downhill and slalom courses.

- Railbars—plastic runners on the underside edges of the skateboard.

- Slalom—a zigzagged racing course with plastic cones.

- Streetstyle—a skateboarding style that uses ramps and stunts.

- Trucks—the metal suspension mechanisms of a skateboard.

- Urethane—a strong type of plastic.